CHRISTMAS GUEST BOOK

GUESTS

GUESTS

_____

_____

_____

GUESTS

GUESTS

_____

_____

_____

_____

GUESTS

GUESTS

_____

_____

_____

_____

GUESTS

GUESTS

GUESTS

GUESTS

_____

_____

_____

_____

_____

_____

_____

_____

_____

_____

_____

_____

_____

_____

_____

_____

_____

_____

_____

GUESTS

_____

_____

_____

_____

GUESTS

_____   _____
                                     _____
                                     _____
                                     _____

_____   _____
                                     _____
                                     _____
                                     _____

_____   _____
                                     _____
                                     _____
                                     _____
                                     _____

_____   _____
                                     _____
                                     _____
                                     _____

GUESTS

_____

_____

_____

GUESTS

GUESTS

GUESTS

_____

_____

_____

_____

GUESTS

GUESTS

GUESTS

GUESTS

_____

_____

GUESTS

_____

_____

_____

_____

GUESTS

_____

_____

_____

_____

GUESTS

GUESTS

_____

_____

_____

_____

GUESTS

GUESTS

GUESTS

GUESTS

GUESTS

GUESTS

_____

_____

_____

_____

GUESTS

GUESTS

GUESTS

GUESTS

GUESTS

GUESTS

_____

_____

_____

_____

GUESTS

GUESTS

GUESTS

GUESTS

_____

_____

_____

_____

GUESTS

GUESTS

_____

_____

_____

_____

GUESTS

GUESTS

_____

_____

_____

_____

_____

_____

_____

_____

_____

_____

_____

_____

_____

_____

_____

_____

_____

_____

GUESTS

GUESTS

_____

_____

_____

_____

GUESTS

GUESTS

GUESTS

GUESTS

_____

_____

_____

_____

GUESTS

GUESTS

GUESTS

GUESTS

GUESTS

GUESTS

GUESTS

GUESTS

GUESTS

GUESTS

GUESTS

GUESTS

GUESTS

GUESTS

GUESTS

_____

_____

_____

_____

GUESTS

_____

_____

_____

_____

GUESTS

GUESTS

_____

_____

_____

_____

GUESTS

GUESTS

_____

_____

_____

_____

_____

_____

_____

_____

_____

_____

_____

_____

_____

_____

_____

_____

_____

_____

_____

GUESTS

GUESTS

GUESTS

GUESTS

GUESTS

GUESTS

GUESTS

GUESTS

GUESTS

GUESTS

_____

_____

_____

_____

_____

_____

_____

_____

_____

_____

_____

_____

_____

_____

_____

_____

_____

_____

_____

_____

GUESTS

GUESTS

_____

_____

_____

_____

GUESTS

GUESTS

GUESTS

GUESTS

_____

_____

_____

_____

GUESTS

GUESTS

GUESTS

GUESTS

_____

_____
_____
_____
_____

_____

_____
_____
_____
_____

_____

_____
_____
_____
_____

_____

_____
_____
_____
_____

GUESTS

GUESTS

GUESTS

GUESTS

_____

_____
_____
_____
_____

_____

_____
_____
_____
_____

_____

_____
_____
_____
_____

_____

_____
_____
_____
_____

GUESTS

GUESTS

_____   _____
                                          _____
                                          _____
                                          _____
                                          _____

_____   _____
                                          _____
                                          _____
                                          _____
                                          _____

_____   _____
                                          _____
                                          _____
                                          _____
                                          _____

_____   _____
                                          _____
                                          _____
                                          _____
                                          _____

GUESTS

Made in the USA
Middletown, DE
08 July 2023

34726809R00057